Whose Fault Is It Anyway?

Earl King

DEDICATION

"Godliness with contentment is great gain."
-I Timothy 6:6

Coach Kenneth Key, together with his wife Cathy, embody a living example of this simple principle. Their lives demonstrate the godly ideal of simplicity that has too often been ignored and even ridiculed in our day. Had our society determined to live by this biblical principle, we would not be facing the financial straits that await us. This book is dedicated to Kenneth and Cathy Key in hopes that many will embrace the same truth that has served them so well and find the same deep contentment they have found.

CONTENTS

Chapter 1

THE BIG QUESTION

There is a train wreck coming. It's an economic train wreck. The United States of America has succeeded in accumulating a national debt so vast that it will be impossible to repay. This is not a theory; it is a fact. At the time of this writing (February 2017), the current national debt of the United States is just short of a dizzying $20 trillion. By the time you read this, it will likely be over $20 trillion.

Once numbers as large as 20,000,000,000,000 are mentioned, it is very easy for eyes to glaze over and interest to wane. We can't really relate to such numbers, so we throw up our hands and think, "Whatever." So let's put this number into perspective. There are approximately 325 million citizens of the United States. If the gross national debt were evenly distributed to every citizen in the United States, then every individual would be approximately $61,500 dollars in debt.

But it gets worse. The debt is very steadily increasing by the second. Anyone who is interested can watch the growth by visiting *usdebtclock.org*. By observing the national debt clock for about 2 minutes, I estimated that the growth is approximately $4,000 per second. Also steadily increasing is the cost to service, or pay interest on, the debt. Currently the US government is paying approximately $450 billion each year in interest alone. With a total US budget of approximately $3.5 trillion, the cost of interest alone is approximately 13% of the budget... and growing. With the inevitable increase in interest rates this nation is soon to face, this 13% figure may grow very significantly in the near future.

If the picture drawn above does not look bleak enough, consider this. Based upon the financial commitments required by the country's Social Security and other entitlement programs, the cost obligations upon the Federal government will be growing much greater in the near future. The vast population of baby boomers will continue to retire and look to Social Security for both retirement benefits and health care benefits. The fact that this burden is unsustainable has been acknowledged by many, but facing this giant has proven a task too politically unpopular for our Federal government to begin to set in place any viable solution. Lawmakers have been content to kick the can down the road. Eventually that road will end.

The national debt is only one portion of the picture. Added to national government debt are state and local government debts. These debts add another $2 – 3 trillion to the total. Then there is personal debt. Recent figures show that each household in America has credit card debt of over $16,000 and total debt of over $130,000. Any effort of the Federal government to reduce the national debt would fly in the face of state and local governments that are already struggling with their own debt issues and families that are already up to their necks in personal debt.

So what do we have? We have an economy that is headed for a very rude awakening. Dare we call it a financial collapse? The question is not IF this will happen; the question is WHEN.

But this book does not attempt to answer the WHEN question. This book only answers the all-important question which will be asked AFTER the collapse: "Whose fault is it anyway?"

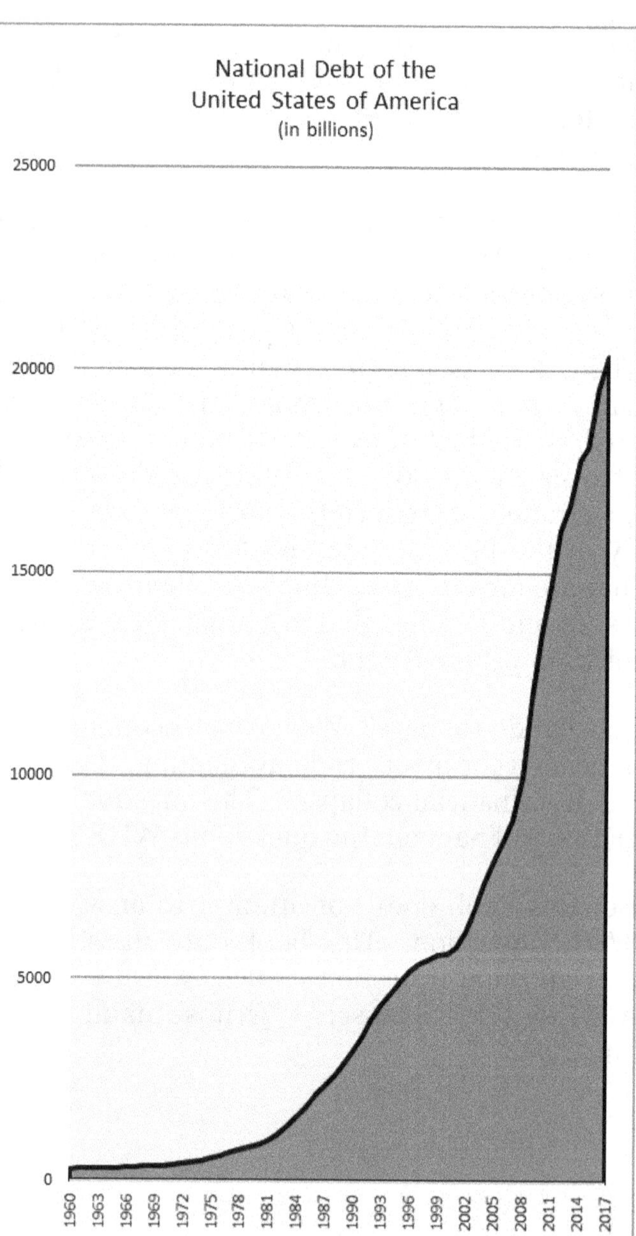

National Debt of the
United States of America
(in billions)
25000
20000
15000
10000
5000
0
1960
1963
1966
1969
1972
1975
1978
1981
1984
1987
1990
1993
1996
1999
2002
2005
2008
2011
2014
2017

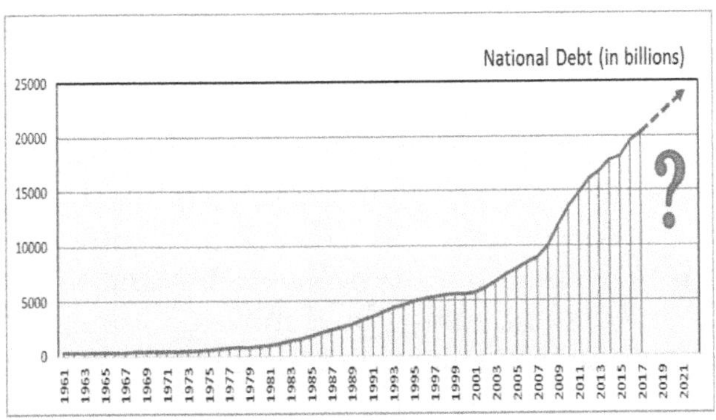

Chapter 2

DONALD TRUMP (2017 –)

Given the dire facts that were stated in the first chapter, it is not unreasonable to predict that the financial crash will take place during the Trump administration. If I am mistaken, I will be glad to write an updated edition of this book four or eight years from now and add a chapter to cover the next President, whoever that may be. For purposes of simplicity, we will assume that the financial collapse takes place during the Trump administration.

What irony it would be if the one who promised to "Make America Great Again" presides over the nation's greatest economic collapse. If the economic forces that continue to display themselves come to a crescendo within the next few years, then that is precisely what will happen.

There will be many who will point their impassioned fingers directly in the face of "the Donald" and declare with confidence, "There is the one who is to blame!" And they will, no doubt, have reason to make that claim. Unlike his predecessors, all seasoned politicians, Trump has no reticence making bold statements and taking bold moves. Supporters and opponents alike would probably agree that Trump is in some ways like a strong bull. His admirers would affirm that he is bullish on America and they hope that his presidency will continue to witness the bullish market that it has enjoyed thus far. His opponents, and there are many, would decry that he is like a bull in a china store, making outlandish statements and championing extreme policies which are sure to upset the status quo and the current world order. His opponents would also feel justified in adding a "y" to the "bull" description.

While his presidency is still too young to be able to affirm much about the eventual financial effects of his actions and policies, such a state of uncertainly will not last forever. The fact that Trump believes in "America first" and has indicated a willingness to engage in protectionist policies may backfire if other nations do the same. Further, his commitment to lower taxes, while increasing military spending, increasing spending on infrastructure, building a giant wall and servicing Americans well through a new health care policy will likely add additional debt.

There is no doubt that – should the crash take place during his presidency – there will be many who will point their fingers at Trump and declare that he is the one to blame for this financial crash. The fine-tuned clockwork of the world economy, many will claim, cannot continue when this outsider so flagrantly disturbs "business as usual."

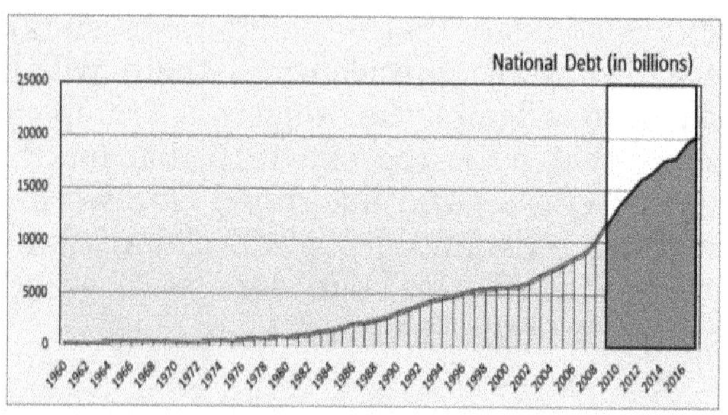

Chapter 3

BARACK OBAMA (2009 – 2017)

Trump and his supporters will certainly not shoulder the blame for the crash. They will point back to his predecessor, Barack Obama. Obama was first elected on the heels of the financial crisis of 2008 and the Great Recession. He inherited a major financial problem, but Trump and others will be quick to point out that he oversaw a gigantic increase of approximately $8 trillion in the national debt. While he could not be blamed for the starting point in 2009, he will certainly be blamed by his detractors for what happened in the ensuing eight years.

The Obama administration considered "stimulus" to be the answer to the financial crisis he inherited. In other words, pump more money into the economy to get it moving. But what money would that be? There was a debt of almost $12 trillion already. There certainly was no reserve that could be used to kick start the economy. Essentially what "stimulus" meant was "more debt." The first few years of the Obama administration witnessed a great deal of stimulus but little improvement. Eventually that changed, and by the time he left office the economy appeared to be getting back on track... at least that's what it looked like to the average American.

Actually things were not quite as rosy as they appeared on the surface. For one thing, though the nation was reducing its annual deficit, it was not reducing its debt. Debt is the total amount that is owed. A deficit, on the other hand, is the amount of debt that is added in any given year. Every year of Obama's administration witnessed a deficit. Each year there was more money spent than collected. What that means is that every year witnessed the nation getting deeper and deeper into debt. However, the speed at which the nation got deeper into debt slowed down. While the first four years witnessed debt increases of almost $5 trillion, the next four years witnessed debt increases of "only" about $3 trillion. At the projected rate of approximately $500 billion a year for the next four years, the nation will be $2 trillion more in debt by 2021.

To put it all in historical perspective, Obama's administration increased the national debt by approximately $8 trillion. The only presidency whose debt enlargement comes even close to that sum is Obama's predecessor, George W. Bush. His eight years witnessed an increase of almost $6 trillion in the national debt.

It may be helpful to those of us who do not have a strong knowledge of economics to use an illustration to understand the difference between deficit and debt. Imagine an airplane whose pilot is having difficulty and finds himself (or herself) unable to cause the airplane to climb. Every second finds the airplane losing altitude. For a while the airplane enters a pattern of descending at a rate of 5,000 feet per minute, but the pilot is able to stabilize the aircraft somewhat so that it is only descending at a rate of 3,000 feet per minute. If you and I were passengers in that airplane, we would probably be very thankful that the rate of descent is not as great now as it had been previously. However, we would certainly not be pleased about the fact that the airplane is still headed down... and fast!

Those who are content to have a lower budget deficit need to realize that the issue is not so much "How quickly are we going down?" as it is "We are still going down!"

There came a point in Obama's administration when the Federal government, finding it more and more difficult to find buyers for its growing debt, actually began buying debt with its own resources, i.e., debt. This caused the country to fall even deeper into debt. Yet this was a type of debt that was reported in a different manner than other debt, making the figures look less dismal.

There was a major indicator that transpired during the Obama administration. For the first time since shortly after World War II, the national debt surpassed the nation's gross domestic product (GPD). Prior to this event, which was realized in 2012, many economists had warned that national debt should not surpass gross domestic product without considerable risk. Having surpassed the GDP, the debt continues to grow at a much faster pace than the GDP, causing the gap between the two to grow greater by the year.

The Trump administration, the Tea Party sympathizers and many right-leaning Americans would have no problem pointing their accusing fingers at Barack Obama as the one to blame for the crash.

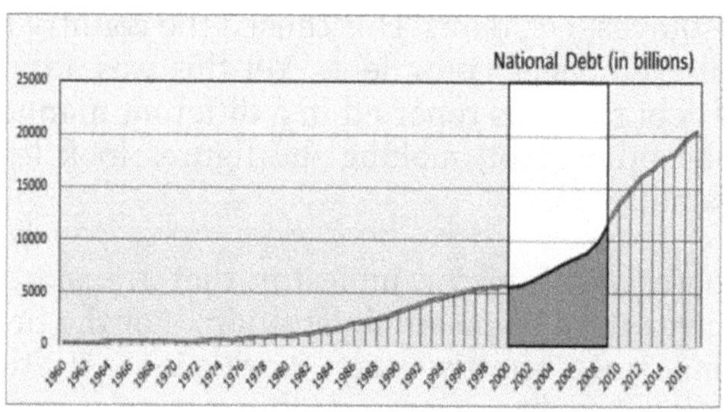

Chapter 4

GEORGE W. BUSH (2001 – 2009)

Barack Obama and his supporters will insist that he is not the one to blame for the financial crash. He inherited a very difficult financial situation from his predecessor, George W. Bush. That "inheritance" included what has come to be known as the Great Recession. The last years of Bush's presidency witnessed major economic downturns. This included plummeting value in real estate in 2006 and 2007, as the real estate market's bubble burst, and a $700 billion payoff in 2008 to keep the economy from completely collapsing.

To make matters more incriminating, unlike Obama, Bush did not inherit a difficult financial situation. At the end of the Clinton presidency and into the first year of his own presidency, the Federal government actually enjoyed a surplus, not a deficit. This changed as Bush dealt with the dotcom bubble burst and as he escalated the war on terror. After 9-11, Bush, riding the crest of the wave of patriotism and national pride, began to mobilize the nation's giant military capabilities to engage the enemy, first in Afghanistan, then in Iraq. It has been estimated that the Iraq War cost America $2 trillion.

Bailouts and war, however, were not the only high-priced expenditures under the Bush administration. Bush approved the vast relief efforts that took place after the 2005 hurricane season, responding to Katrina, Rita and Wilma. Approximately $100 billion was appropriated for these efforts. Though $100 billion may seem small compared to the $2 trillion cost for the Iraq War, this expenditure represents a deeper reality with ongoing repercussions. Americans have come to expect that the Federal government has an obligation to its citizens to come to their rescue in times of disaster. The apparent reticence of George W's father to "dispatch the cavalry" following Hurricane Andrew may have ultimately cost him the election in 1992. Younger Bush learned a big political lesson from the incident, which he was careful to avoid in 2005.

The importance of "social spending" in the George W. Bush administration is very significant in America's race to bankruptcy. Traditionally it has been the Democrats who have championed social spending – spending that is designed to aid the needy in society, whether it be the poor, the disadvantaged, the disabled, or the elderly. From the beginning, Bush projected himself as a Republican who supports social spending. Without doing so, no doubt he would have lost the election to Al Gore, considering the fact the election was ultimately decided by the narrowest of margins – a few hundred votes in Florida. During the televised debates with Gore, it was Bush who proposed a very un-Republican answer to the question of what to do with the tax surplus that had accumulated under the Clinton administration. His plan: give it back to the people in the form of refund checks. In so doing he won the election, but he changed the dynamics of the economic debate in America. Whereas it used to be that the Republicans emphasized a strong defense while the Democrats emphasized social spending, Bush embraced both. Republicans have tended to stress fiscal responsibility, at the expense of being accused of being uncompassionate. Bush turned from that emphasis. Politically that was a wise move, but the economic consequences are being experienced today. It is one thing to embrace both military spending and social spending when you have money to spend. It is another thing altogether to do so at the expense of rising national debt.

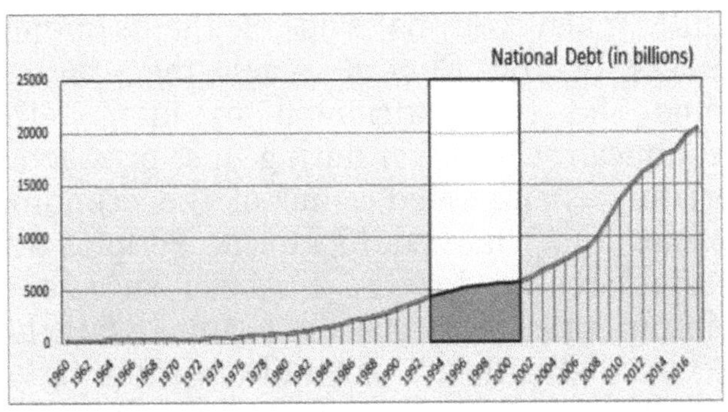

Chapter 5

BILL CLINTON (1993 – 2001)

From an economic standpoint, it would appear on the surface that – of all presidents to blame – Clinton may be the least deserving. After all, when he was inaugurated in 1993, his predecessor, George H.W. Bush had overseen the racking up of approximately $1.4 trillion in debt in only one term. In two terms Clinton oversaw the net rise in debt of "only" about $1.4 trillion, cutting the rate of rush into debt by 50%. The last two years of his presidency actually witnessed budget surpluses – the only surplus years since 1969. Clinton presided over what some economists claim was the longest economic expansion in the nation's history. He also passed long-term reduction in social spending, further easing budgetary concerns. It would appear as if Clinton stands out as the one president who reversed the rising tide of deficit spending.

While much can be said of the economic success of the Clinton years, that success cannot be fully attributed to him. The Republican Congress during his presidency certainly championed some of the economic policies that marked his term. Perhaps the greatest reason for the financial success of Clinton's presidency was the fortunate fact that it coincided with the dawn of the Information Age. The United States, supported by such big players as Microsoft and Apple, led the way in the worldwide transition from the Industrial Age to the Information Age. The coinciding of the beginning of this mammoth transformation with the Clinton administration had little to do with the latter, rumors of Al Gore "inventing" the Internet notwithstanding.

Clinton's detractors would point to other problems in his economic legacy. There were major policy moves made during Clinton's presidency that his detractors claim paved the way for the extreme financial problems the country now faces. Bush supporters would complain that, while Clinton's term reaped the benefits of the dotcom bubble, it was Bush's term that was left holding the bag when the bubble burst. Others would claim that the deregulations in financing that were passed in the Clinton years were largely responsible for the major financing collapse that inaugurated the Great Recession. Others would claim that Clinton's free trade policies have resulted in the massive movement of the nation's industry to other countries. By selling the goose that laid the golden eggs, the ongoing prosperity of the nation, they claim, was jeopardized.

That the economy fared well during the Clinton years is undeniable. Whether or not Clinton's policies ultimately resulted in detrimental consequences to the nation's economy is debatable.

A note must also be made of the difference between deficit and debt. Though the deficits in the last three years of the Clinton budgets were replaced by surpluses, the national debt actually continued to grow during every year of the Clinton administration. This took place because the nation continued to "borrow" from Social Security to make budget ends meet. Altogether, the Clinton administration witnessed a national debt increase of approximately $1.4 trillion, over 30% of the $4.4 trillion debt that he inherited.

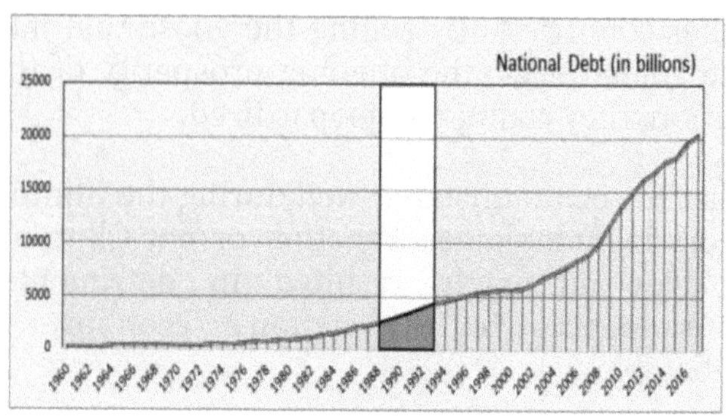

Chapter 6

GEORGE H. W. BUSH (1989 – 1993)

"Voodoo economics." This was the term that George H. W. Bush, the Republican candidate for president in 1980, used during the Republican presidential primary to describe the proposed economic model that his Republican opponent, Ronald Reagan, championed. That model was more precisely, and less derogatively, called "supply-side" economics. Essentially this is the theory that the more you cut taxes, the more the economy will grow, producing more tax revenue at these lower tax rates than would otherwise have been collected at higher tax rates.

Despite his opposition to Reagan's economics, Bush was willing to climb on board the Reagan ticket, which proved successful in claiming the presidency. He had little choice throughout the

8 years of the Reagan era than to go along with the economic policies of his boss. By the end of the second term, the nation as a whole was very pleased with the way in which the nation was headed. On the foreign scene it appeared as if the Reagan team had essentially won the Cold War, and on the domestic scene the economy seemed to be moving along relatively smoothly. When Bush took office in 1989 he was not about to rock the boat, economically or otherwise.

Bush continued down the road that Reagan had blazed. While the supply-side model had promised that taxes would be able to maintain the needed supply of revenue, even at lower rates, the model actually resulted in deficits. Bush inherited a budget debt of less than $3 trillion. By the end of his term it had grown by approximately $1.4 trillion to well over $4 trillion. His one term in office increased the Federal budget by a greater amount than any term of any president before him.

What accounted for this extensive increase in debt? Less than $100 billion of this total cost can be attributed to the Gulf War. Over $100 billion was used to bail out the savings and loans institutions that crumbled during his tenure. The cost in interest on debt also became increasingly significant, making it the third-largest item in the Federal budget after defense and Social Security. By increasing the Federal debt there is automatically a bill in interest payments that is passed down to future taxpayers.

Perhaps the greatest factor causing the tremendous deficits of the Bush term resulted from the political struggle with Congress. In Bush's election bid he needed the support of the Reaganomics believers, so he promised "No new taxes!" He expected pushback from Democrats but insisted that he would rebuff their insistence upon higher taxes: "Read my lips: No new taxes!" He was hopeful that he could make extensive cuts in the domestic budget in order to balance the Federal budget. The Democratic Congress in power at the time was not willing to make such concessions, resulting in high expenditures and "no new taxes," a clear recipe for budget deficits. His eventual agreement to backtrack on his promise and allow for new taxes proved to be an affront to his support base and a contributing factor in his failure to attain reelection.

The bailout of the failing savings and loan industry set a precedent for the future that would come back to haunt his son in 2008 when the same reasoning was used to bailout the nation's banking system at the much higher price tag of $700 billion.

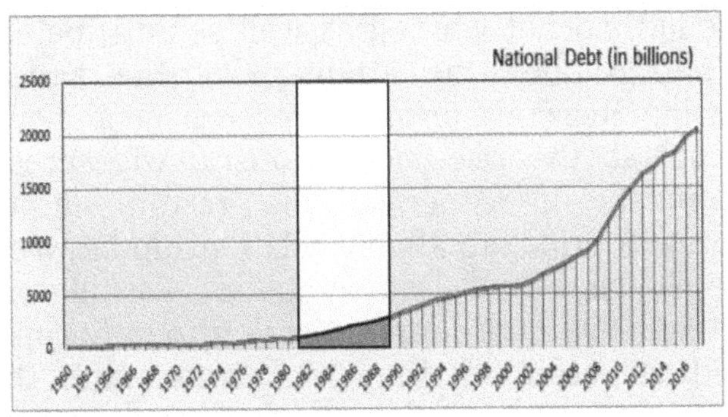

Chapter 7

RONALD REAGAN (1981 – 1989)

Though Bush himself may be too loyal to the Reagan camp do so, he certainly would have reason to point back to his predecessor as the one ultimately to blame for the eventual collapse of the nation's economy under the heavy weight of debt. History may eventually attest to the accuracy of Bush's initial assessment of Reaganomics: "voodoo economics." While there is no doubt some value in stimulating the economy by lowering taxes, history has demonstrated that this strategy has its limits, which must not be discounted.

At Reagan's inauguration, the national debt was less than $1 trillion; when he left office eight years later, it was nearing $3 trillion. It would certainly appear as if the supply-side model had not worked as well as anticipated. What grabbed the attention of the nation during Reagan's terms were such good news items as the rise in patriotism, widespread optimism in America, the restoration of national pride, an affable relationship between Republicans and Democrats in Washington, the weakening of communism's grip in Europe, and an economy that was overcoming the inflation and malaise of the previous administration. What was not given a great deal of attention at the time was the Federal debt. Though Reagan made some definite gains in the economy over his eight years as president, he did so at the expense of almost tripling the national debt.

Much of the increased debt during the Reagan years and other presidencies before and after him stemmed from "borrowing" from the nation's Social Security fund. This was one fund that was robust at the time Reagan took office. From a practical perspective, no one would feel the difference of these borrowed funds for many years to come. With each president after him continuing the same strategy, it is now undeniable that there is coming a day when Social Security will no longer be able to bear the weight of its promised commitments.

History has tended to look favorably on the Reagan presidency. On the international scene, Reagan's strong leadership exerted an influence that helped bring an end to the Cold War. On the domestic scene his administration oversaw the reduction in runaway inflation and unemployment, forging a strong economic recovery. Many who value free market policies, reduced government interference in the economy and tax reduction point to the Reagan years as strong proof of the efficacy of these values. Others who are more concerned with class inequity and the taming of big business would stress its failure on these fronts. Regardless of these varying perspectives, one observation that can be made concerning the Reagan years is that they mark an acceptance of large and sustained deficit spending. This acceptance perpetuated the long, monumental climb of national debt for the following decades in American history, a trend that has steadily been gaining momentum.

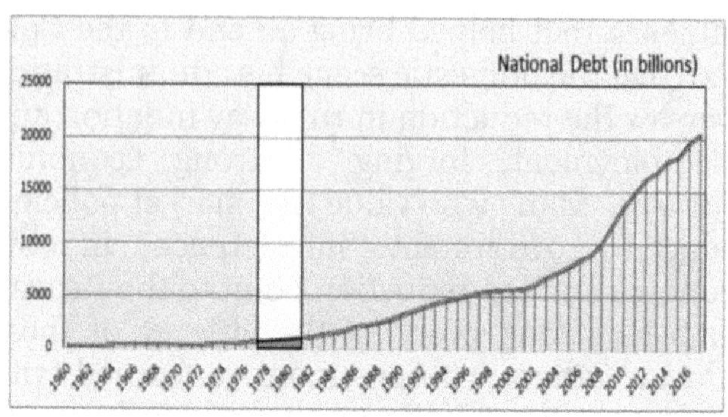

Chapter 8

JIMMY CARTER (1977 – 1981)

Reagan admirers would be very quick to point out the fact that Reagan inherited a very dismal economy from his predecessor, Jimmy Carter. Carter's administration had the dubious distinction of overseeing an economy characterized by both high inflation and high unemployment. The high inflation especially threatened to undermine the nation's economy for years to come.

As of this day, it would appear as if history has not looked very favorably upon the Carter administration. One reason for this general consensus is the perception that he was not a strong leader. He seemed to be more concerned about insuring that there is a good process for decision-making than he was about providing clear direction and moving forward with a clearly-defined strategy. The term malaise is often used to describe the nation and its economy under the Carter administration.

Perhaps of much greater significance than the leadership style of Carter himself were the significant external challenges that took place during his term of office. Though it is undeniable that inflation spiked during his term of office, the reasons for that spike were not of his making. When the government of Iran was overthrown by a radical Islamic faction, the supply of oil to the nation was immediately curtailed. Reduced supply resulted in higher oil prices, which in turn resulted in higher prices for other goods and services. This inflation was comparable to the inflation experienced when oil prices skyrocketed in late 1973 under the Nixon administration.

To his credit, Carter nominated Paul Volker for the Chairman of the Federal Reserve Board. Through his very unpopular policy of vastly raising the borrowing rates, the nation was thrust into a recession in the short run, followed by a 7-year recovery in the long run. Of course Carter was not in power long enough to enjoy the recovery part of this successful strategy. He was willing to hurt himself politically in the short run in order to benefit the country in the long run.

The increase of the national debt during the

Carter administration was significant. His administration added approximately $300 billion to the national debt, increasing it by over 40%.

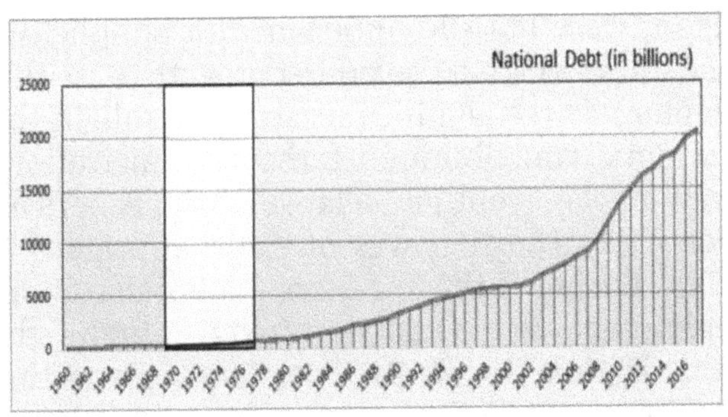

Chapter 9

RICHARD NIXON &
GERALD FORD (1969 – 1977)

While campaigning for President against incumbent Gerald Ford, Carter emphasized the claim that the nation's economy under Ford was poor. He pointed to the "misery index," the sum of the unemployment and inflation rates, as proof of this. Under Ford and Nixon, the misery index reached the highest number under any US President: 13.57 was the number Carter highlighted in the summer of 1976. When casting blame, Carter advocates will be quick to point out that he inherited an economy that was in deep trouble to begin with. (Carter advocates would prefer not to point out that at the close of his administration the "misery index" had risen to over 19.)

Because Ford and his predecessor, Richard

Nixon, were both Republicans, for simplicity's sake they will be considered together in this chapter. Three significant factors highlight the economic contributions these administrations made to the eventual collapse of the American economy. The first was of external origin. It was during the Nixon administration, beginning in October 1973, that the Organization of Arab Petroleum Exporting Countries (OAPEC) proclaimed an oil embargo on the United States and some of its allies for support of Israel during the Yom Kippur war in 1973. As a result, oil prices quadrupled, resulting in exceptionally high inflation throughout the country.

The other two significant factors were of internal origin. The Nixon administration, in an attempt to win "peace with honor" in the Vietnam War, escalated the war effort in the early years of his administration, resulting in substantial debt. As the war wound down, some of the financial commitments that had been earmarked for military spending were shifted to domestic spending in the entitlements that the Johnson administration had inaugurated. Bottom line: debt grew significantly under the Nixon/Ford administrations.

The third major factor during the Nixon/Ford administrations was perhaps the most significant of all in the long run for national debt growth. On August 15, 1971, Nixon shocked the world when he announced that the United States would no longer tie the value of the US dollar to the gold standard. A monetary system that had been in effect for almost 25 years was abandoned. Had the nation continued to be bound to the gold standard, its debt would have been essentially limited by its gold reserves. With the national currency no longer tied to a limiting factor of actual gold in reserve, the stage was set for essentially unlimited growth in the national debt. The initial result of Nixon's decision was minimal; the eventual result has proven monumental.

All told, national debt mushroomed under the Nixon/Ford administrations by approximately $340 billion, over 90%, from the $365 billion inherited from the Johnson administration.

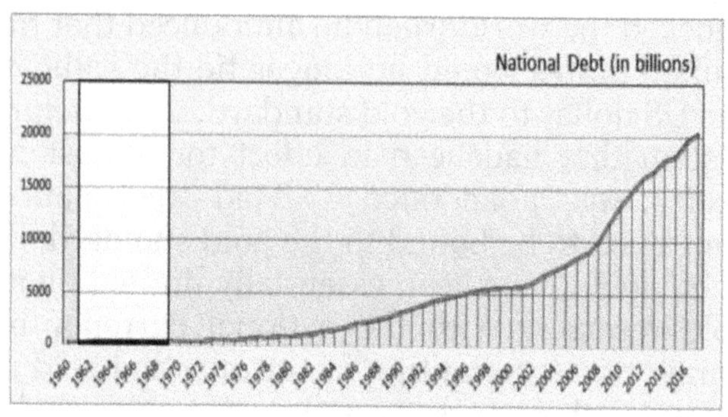

Chapter 10

JOHN F. KENNEDY &
LYNDON B. JOHNSON (1961 – 1969)

Nixon admirers will point back to the previous Democratic presidencies of John F. Kennedy and Lyndon B. Johnson as the real culprits in the economic slide of the nation into unsustainable national debt. After all, one of the most pressing economic issues that Nixon had to face was the Vietnam War. He did not start this war; he inherited it from the previous administrations. Furthermore, the previous administrations had laid the foundations for vastly increased domestic spending through its "war on poverty." With Johnson's "Great Society" came a great cost intrinsically woven into the fabric of the nation's DNA.

From a humanitarian perspective, much can be said in support of the combined efforts of

Kennedy and Johnson to assist the most disadvantaged within the American society, including the mentally ill, the poor in general and the black poor in particular. From a purely financial perspective, however, detractors would point to the Kennedy/Johnson administrations as the ones most responsible for instilling and developing an "entitlement" orientation whereby citizens look to government as an institution tasked with assisting them with financial aid whenever there is financial need. In the short-term, the domestic cost to the national economy was small in comparison with the cost of the Vietnam War. In the long-term, however, this cost has proven much greater. An entitlement-oriented citizenry, not limited to the poor and disadvantaged but encompassing the whole populace, has resulted in national obligations that continue to grow until their unsustainable nature causes eventual collapse.

Kennedy's inaugural speech in 1961 is most remembered for his challenge to the citizens of America: "Ask not what your country can do for you. Ask what you can do for your country." It is ironic that the judgment of history may be that the Kennedy/Johnson administrations resulted in a perspective that – more than any other administrations – fostered the opposite: "Ask not what you can do for your country. Ask what your country can do for you."

All told, the combined effect of the Kennedy/Johnson administrations was to increase the national debt by approximately $73 billion, or 25%.

32

Chapter 11

THE ANSWER

For purposes of answering the question, "Whose fault is it anyway?" we will not look any further back in history than the Kennedy/Johnson administrations. Interestingly, with 7 terms each, the Democrats and Republicans evenly divided presidential power for the 56 years between 1961 and 2017. Furthermore, with approximately $10 trillion each, the Democrats and Republicans contributed roughly the same sum of national debt over these 56 years.

So whose fault is it anyway?

Blame cannot be placed on any one President or administration. Neither can blame be placed on any one party. To understand whose fault it really is for the fact that this nation, which once boasted the greatest economy in history, has now accumulated so much debt that a crash is inevitable, we need only read the first three words of the Preamble to the Unites States Constitution: "We the People..."

In a monarchy or a dictatorship, blame can easily and rightly be placed upon the nation's ruler. In a democracy, however, "We the People" are ultimately the ones who determine what course we choose to take. "We the People" elect our Presidents, our congresses, many of our judges, and our local governments. "We the People" determine what direction we would like our government to go and ultimately how we would like to spend our government's money. If one candidate or party does not please us, "We the People" have the power to change course. When we point an accusing finger at any one President or party, three fingers point back to ourselves. We have no one to blame for the coming crash but ourselves.

Chapter 12

WHAT HAPPENED?

So what happened? What got us to this point? How could we have squandered a robust economy for an economy that is on the brink of collapse? Where did we go off track?

Approximately 40 years ago, one of our presidents gave an address to the American people, sounding an alarm. Unfortunately we did not heed the alarm. On July 15, 1979, during the national oil crisis, President Jimmy Carter addressed the nation. While he challenged the American people to embrace energy conservation, he highlighted something much deeper and more ominous:

I want to talk to you right now about a fundamental threat to American democracy... I do not refer to the outward strength of America, a nation that is at peace tonight everywhere in the world, with unmatched economic power and military might. The threat is nearly invisible in ordinary ways....

In a nation that was proud of hard work, strong families, close-knit communities, and our faith in God, too many of us now tend to worship self-indulgence and consumption. Human identity is no longer defined by what one does, but by what one owns. But we've discovered that owning things and consuming things does not satisfy our longing for meaning....

The basic underlying issue that Carter observed in its infancy 40 years ago has matured and grown until now it has completely imbedded itself in our society. There are many different words that can be used to describe the problem: self-indulgence... materialism... consumerism.... Or you can call it by its good old-fashioned name: greed. Our nation has embraced greed. "We the People" have become greedy. Greed is never satisfied. If always wants more. It is not content with a higher standard of living than virtually any other nation in the world; it must have more. Whether it's a bigger house, or a nicer car, or a more lavish vacation, or a higher salary, or a newer phone, or a more stylish wardrobe, or a swankier restaurant experience, or a more expressive hairdo, or a thousand other things, greed is never content. Because we are greedy, we spend even when we cannot afford to spend. We spend beyond our means, and so go into debt. This same willingness to spend more than we can afford is passed on from "We the People" to our government and our nation. "We the People" are responsible for the bankruptcy that our nation is on the verge of experiencing because of our greed.

Closely aligned to greed is its partner in crime: *pride*. Often the reason that we want more is because we want to exalt ourselves above our neighbors. Not only do we want to keep up with the Joneses, we want to do better than the Joneses. We like the recognition that comes with conspicuous consumption. We are willing to pay more for products not because the products are so much better but because they are so much more prestigious, screaming, "Look at what I am able to spend!" As "We the People" have fueled our greed by our pride, so we have done as a nation. Much of the intensity behind our spending, whether it be for such divergent causes as maintaining our status as the world's greatest military power or forging our status as a strong force against climate change, can be traced to pride.

Greed and pride are deeply ingrained in our character as a nation and as a people. We speak of "the American dream" as if it is a cherished ideal that all should aspire to achieve. But what is "the American dream" but a goal in materialistic pursuit? Our dream is not to be better people or more godly individuals. Our dream is to own our own castles and fulfill our own materialistic goals. We splatter our streets and public places with commercials for things and billboards to entice us to achieve ever greater degrees of materialistic achievements. Even our tee shirts advertise products and services that urge us to spend more. Our omnipresent televisions and social media technologies broadcast and stream commercials incessantly, carefully crafted by Madison Avenue corporations to further fuel our addiction to *more* and *better*.

We are proud to be Americans. National pride is often touted as a singular virtue. In our zeal to appreciate our blessed nation, which is certainly commendable, we have sometimes embraced an extreme and haughty conceit that looks down on other nationalities and struts about as if we are somehow better than others, which is certainly deplorable.

Whose fault is it anyway? We have no one President to blame, no political party to blame, no one to blame but ourselves. We all share to some degree blame for the bleak fate that awaits us. This author does not exclude himself from this judgment. "We the People of the United States of America" are to blame for the coming economic crash because we have embraced greed and pride.

Chapter 13

COMING HOME

I don't know exactly what the coming financial crisis will look like. Will it be characterized by widespread unemployment, or runaway inflation or both? Will it be as devastating as the Great Depression? Will America ever return to its current level of economic prosperity? I do not know. What I do know is that it will hurt. We as a people will realize a degree of financial distress that most of us have never experienced or even imagined. There will be no quick fix. There will be a new normal that will not be nearly as comfortable as the current normal.

This chapter is intended to address the many who will be greatly impacted by the coming economic crash. Not only is there hope, but there will be an amazing opportunity which, if embraced, can transform this monumental disappointment into a glorious new beginning.

Jesus told a story that we have come to know as the Parable of the Prodigal Son. It tells of a son who, unwilling to wait until his father died, asked his father to give him his inheritance now. Soon after receiving it he set off for a far country and proceeded to squander all the money on wild living. After spending everything, there was a famine in the land and he came into great need. He found himself with the menial task of feeding pigs, and he was so hungry that he longed to eat their slop.

Only when he dipped to this low point did the son "come to his senses." He realized that his father's servants lived much better than he was living. So he decided to go home to his father and admit that he had been wrong. He had sinned both against heaven and against the father. He would ask to be received back as a hired servant. The impoverished and penitent son must have been practicing his speech to his father on the long road home. Yet while he was still a long way off, the father saw him and was filled with compassion for him. The father ran to him, embraced him and kissed him. Before the son could finish his speech, the father ordered that the best robe be placed on him, together with a ring and sandals. He ordered a feast and began a great celebration. He received him back joyfully, not as a servant but as a son.

We as a nation have gone the way of the prodigal son. Rather than pursuing God, we have set our hearts on wealth and material things. When those things are gone, we will realize how empty they were and how spiritually bankrupt we have become. When we get to that low point, we as a people will have the opportunity to "come to our senses" and return to our Heavenly Father. And when we do so, we will find that He not only allows us to come home, but He will treat us as long-lost children.

A great blessing is awaiting this nation. It is not financial prosperity. Our experience has taught us that that financial prosperity does not satisfy our deepest longings. We have found that greed is never satisfied. The blessing that awaits us is our return to the Father. There we will find joys much deeper than the shallow pleasures of owning things. We will find spiritual wealth much greater and more satisfying than material goods. We will find fulfillment much more profound than all the money in the world could offer. We will find riches much more permanent than mere gold that perishes. We will find home.

ABOUT THE AUTHOR

Earl King's circuitous career has included experience as a construction worker, landscaper, elementary school teacher, Bible college professor, pastor, operations manager, civil servant and consultant. He has authored two other books: *Whatever Happened to Western Civilization?* and *God's Amazing Christmas Pageant.* He resides with his wife, Cathy, in Coconut Creek, Florida.